I Didn't Know I Was A BULLY

Six Literature-Based Lessons On Bullying Behaviors

WRITTEN BY
Melissa Crawford Richards

ILLUSTRATED BY
JEFFREY ZWARTJES

DEDICATION

I dedicate this book to my family. Lance, you are the rock in my life and my best friend. Jarod and Jessica, you make my days shine. Your support and ideas have been a tremendous help.

I DIDN'T KNOW I WAS A BULLY

10-DIGIT ISBN: 1-57543-138-6   13-DIGIT ISBN: 978-1-57543-138-3

REPRINTED 2007, 2009
COPYRIGHT © 2006 MAR✶CO PRODUCTS, INC.
   Published by mar✶co products, inc.
   1443 Old York Road
   Warminster, PA 18974
   1-800-448-2197
   www.marcoproducts.com

PERMISSION TO REPRODUCE: The purchaser may reproduce the activity sheets, free and without special permission, for participant use for a particular group or class. Reproduction of these materials for an entire school system is forbidden.

All rights reserved. Except as provided above, no part of this book may be reproduced or transmitted in whole or in part in any form or by any means, electronic or mechanical, including photocopying, recording, or by any information storage or retrieval system without permission in writing by the publisher.

PRINTED IN THE U.S.A.

CONTENTS

INTRODUCTION 6
   PRE/POST-TEST EVALUATION 8

ASCA STANDARDS 9

I DIDN'T KNOW I WAS A BULLY (STORY) 11

LESSONS 33

   LESSON 1: BULLYING 34
      BEHAVIOR REFLECTIONS 38

   LESSON 2: BULLYING 39
      IN THE SHOW 43
      CHOOSING SIDES 44

   LESSON 3: BULLYING 45
      IT'S JUST FUNNY 50
      FRIENDSHIP FEARS 51

   LESSON 4: BULLYING 53
      THE CYBERBULLY 57
      I WASN'T THE BULLY 59

   LESSON 5: BULLYING 60
      IN THE SHOW 63
      BEHAVIOR-CHANGE STEPS 65
      BEHAVIOR-CHANGE WORKSHEET 66

   LESSON 6: BULLYING 67
      BOB THE BULLY CARD GAME CENTER INSTRUCTIONS 69
      BULLYING BULLETIN BOARD CENTER INSTRUCTIONS 75
      BULLYING BOOK CENTER INSTRUCTIONS 77
      BULLYING WEB SEARCH CENTER INSTRUCTIONS 79
      BULLYING BEHAVIOR TIC-TAC-TOE CENTER INSTRUCTIONS 81
      BULLYING WORD SEARCH CENTER INSTRUCTIONS 86
      BULLYING CROSSWORD PUZZLE CENTER INSTRUCTIONS 89
      BULLYING FILMSTRIP CENTER INSTRUCTIONS 92

SUPPLEMENTARY ACTIVITY PAGES 95
- SUPPLEMENTARY PAGE INSTRUCTIONS/SUGGESTIONS 96
- I DON'T WANT TO BE A BULLY RAP 98
- BULLIES, BULLIES EVERYWHERE 99
- BULLYING BEHAVIOR GRID 100
- HIDDEN BULLYING MESSAGE 102
- BULLYING SKIT PROMPTS 103
- TEASING/LAUGHING 104
- EXCLUDING 105
- FRIENDSHIP BULLYING 106
- CYBERBULLYING 107
- BEHAVIOR-CHANGE PLAN 108
- BEHAVIOR-CHANGE LOG 109
- BEHAVIOR SURVEY 110

ABOUT THE AUTHOR 112

INTRODUCTION

I Didn't Know I Was A Bully is a program that approaches this pertinent topic not from the viewpoint of the victim or the bystander as so many publications do, but from the viewpoint of the *bully*. Many people bully others and do not realize that they are bullies. That is because many seemingly nonthreatening behaviors are overlooked. Yet these behaviors hurt others. This program helps students identify these seemingly insignificant behaviors and recognize the bullying behaviors they themselves exhibit. The intent of this program is not only to help students identify these behaviors, but also to learn how these behaviors damage relationships with others.

People can change their behavior. Once identified and acknowledged, behaviors can be altered. *I Didn't Know I Was A Bully* helps students begin to monitor their own actions and learn and and utilize social behaviors that will strengthen friendships. *I Didn't Know I Was A Bully* uses positive peer pressure to help students alter negative behaviors. Once children understand the behavioral expectations of others, bullying will become socially unacceptable.

Bullies are not just insecure people without friends. They are sometimes very confident and driven by the need for power. Bullies may be friends who believe they need to have total control in their relationships. Teaching young bullies how to change these behaviors will help them grow up to be adults who enjoy positive relationships.

I Didn't Know I Was A Bully teaches strategies victims and bystanders can use in dealing with bullying. Students learn to confront the bully in a nonthreatening way. If this is unsuccessful, they are encouraged to seek help from an adult. Students are taught that relationships require work. Everyone has and will encounter a bully and must learn strategies for dealing with bullies throughout life.

How To Use
I Didn't Know I Was A Bully

I Didn't Know I Was A Bully can be used in Kindergarten through Grade 5 by selecting those components which address the grade level to which the program is being presented.

The story, *I Didn't Know I Was A Bully* (pages 11-32), is the foundation of the program and can be used at all levels. The story can be reproduced by the purchaser of the book for his/her student groups or read by the leader to the students. How the story is used depends on the maturity level of the students and is the leader's choice. The six lessons and *Supplementary Activities* are applicable for Grades 3-5.

Kindergarten-Grade 2: Read the story before making the presentation. Note any pages you would like to eliminate and any words the children may not understand or may need clarification. Decide on the number of lessons you wish to devote to the story and divide the chosen pages into that number of lessons. Distribute a copy of the story and crayons to each student. Read the selected pages, relate the illustrations to the text, discuss the story with the students, then allow them to color the illustrations.

Grades 3-5: *I Didn't Know I Was A Bully* is divided into six lessons to be presented to students in Grades 3-5. The sixth lesson is in a "center format" and may be expanded to additional sessions. The program may be presented as classroom guidance lessons or during small-group counseling sessions.

Written to be presented in sequential order, the lessons deal with bullying situations that students face regularly. Each of the lessons begins with the objectives to be taught, a list of the required materials, and a description of any necessary pre-presentation preparation. The lesson itself includes a short story, accompanying discussion questions, and follow-up activities. *Supplementary Activities* (pages 95-110) are provided to enhance a lesson or to extend the program into additional lessons.

Evaluating The Program

When implementing a curriculum, it is important to measure the growth students have made. By administering pre- and post-tests, the facilitator can determine which skills have been learned and mastered and which, if any, need to be reinforced for an individual or the entire class.

Monitoring a program also provides validation for the facilitator. It demonstrates that the facilitator is evaluating his/her own classroom performance.

A *Pre/Post-Test Evaluation* for Grades 3-5 is included in the program (page 8). Those who wish to reproduce this test for their students may do so. Administer the test prior to starting the program and at the conclusion of the lessons. The evaluation may be adapted by the facilitator for use with Kindergarten-Grade 2.

ANSWER KEY

Fill In The Blank

1. identify
2. negative
3. non-verbal
4. Excluding
5. friendship
6. power
7. you
8. I-messages
9. victim
10. bystander
11. cyberbullying
12. stop
13. adult
14. plan
15. amends

True/False

1. False
2. True
3. False
4. True
5. False
6. True
7. False
8. False
9. False
10. False

I DIDN'T KNOW I WAS A BULLY
PRE/POST-TEST EVALUATION

NAME_____ DATE_____

Read each sentence and use the following words to fill the blanks.

victim	friendship	identify	you	stop	adult
plan	amends	negative	power	bystander	Excluding
I-messages	non-verbal	cyberbullying			

1. The first step in changing behavior is to _____ the behavior.
2. Bullying is a _____ or unacceptable behavior.
3. Tone of voice and the look on a person's face are examples of _____ messages.
4. _____ means leaving others out on purpose to show power over them.
5. "I'm not going to be your friend if … " is an example of _____ bullying.
6. Friendship _____ should be equal.
7. When a friend tries to control you, it's okay to remind your friend that _____ control you.
8. _____ tell others how you feel about what they are doing and what you want them to do.
9. The target of a bully is called a _____ .
10. The person who witnesses bullying is called a _____ .
11. Sending negative messages about another person on the computer is called _____ .
12. It is okay to ask a friend to _____ bullying another person.
13. An _____ may need to be told about repeated bullying.
14. You can come up with a _____ to change your behavior.
15. You can apologize or make _____ for negative behavior toward others.

Read the statement and circle **TRUE** or **FALSE**.

1. Bullies are only people who become physical and harm others.   TRUE   FALSE
2. Being aware of what you say to others and how you say it can keep you from being a bully.   TRUE   FALSE
3. Friends are never bullies.   TRUE   FALSE
4. Telling someone how you feel is okay.   TRUE   FALSE
5. Bullies are always people who are lonely and insecure.   TRUE   FALSE
6. Bullies can change their behavior.   TRUE   FALSE
7. Being a bully is cool.   TRUE   FALSE
8. People should mind their own business when a bully is picking on a victim.   TRUE   FALSE
9. If you are upset with a friend, you should keep your feelings a secret.   TRUE   FALSE
10. Telling an adult about bullying is *tattling* and should not be done.   TRUE   FALSE

I DIDN'T KNOW I WAS A BULLY
ASCA STANDARDS

PERSONAL/SOCIAL DEVELOPMENT

Standard A: Students will acquire the knowledge, attitudes and interpersonal skills to help them understand and respect self and others.

PS:A1	**Acquire Self-Knowledge**
PS:A1.1	Develop positive attitudes toward self as a unique and worthy person
PS:A1.2	Identify values, attitudes and beliefs
PS:A1.3	Learn the goal-setting process
PS:A1.4	Understand change is a part of growth
PS:A1.5	Identify and express feelings
PS:A1.6	Distinguish between appropriate and inappropriate behavior
PS:A1.7	Recognize personal boundaries, rights and privacy needs
PS:A1.8	Understand the need for self-control and how to practice it
PS:A1.9	Demonstrate cooperative behavior in groups
PS:A1.10	Identify personal strengths and assets
PS:A1.11	Identify and discuss changing personal and social roles

PS:A2	**Acquire Interpersonal Skills**
PS:A2.1	Recognize that everyone has rights and responsibilities
PS:A2.2	Respect alternative points of view
PS:A2.3	Recognize, accept, respect and appreciate individual differences
PS:A2.4	Recognize, accept and appreciate ethnic and cultural diversity
PS:A2.5	Recognize and respect differences in various family configurations
PS:A2.6	Use effective communications skills
PS:A2.7	Know that communication involves speaking, listening and nonverbal behavior
PS:A2.8	Learn how to make and keep friends

Standard B: Students will make decisions, set goals and take necessary action to achieve goals.

PS:B1	**Self-Knowledge Application**
PS:B1.1	Use a decision-making and problem-solving model
PS:B1.2	Understand consequences of decisions and choices
PS:B1.3	Identify alternative solutions to a problem
PS:B1.4	Develop effective coping skills for dealing with problems
PS:B1.5	Demonstrate when, where and how to seek help for solving problems and making decisions
PS:B1.6	Know how to apply conflict resolution skills
PS:B1.7	Demonstrate a respect and appreciation for individual and cultural differences
PS:B1.8	Know when peer pressure is influencing a decision
PS:B1.10	Identify alternative ways of achieving goals
PS:B1.12	Develop an action plan to set and achieve realistic goals

Standard C: Students will understand safety and survival skills.

PS:C1	**Acquire Personal Safety Skills**
PS:C1.5	Differentiate between situations requiring peer support and situations requiring adult professional help
PS:C1.6	Identify resource people in the school and community, and know how to seek their help
PS:C1.10	Learn techniques for managing stress and conflict
PS:C1.11	Learn coping skills for managing life events

I thought a bully was the older boy who stole your lunch money.

I didn't know I was a bully when I wouldn't let you sit at my lunch table.

I didn't know I was a bully when I made you worry instead of letting you do your homework.

I didn't know I was a bully when I rolled my eyes to your face.

I thought a bully was someone who said he or she was going to hurt you.

I didn't know I was a bully when I sent you hurtful messages by excluding you.

I didn't know I was a bully when I wrote bad things about you on the computer.

— don't tell Ashley -- she's a blabbermouth. >:<

I didn't know I was a bully if I laughed when others made fun of you.

I didn't know I was a bully when I thought I was "leader of the pack."

We thought other people were bullies.

We didn't know WE were acting like bullies.

LESSON 1
BULLYING

Objective:

To present the topic of *bullying* and to teach the children to understand and identify bullying behaviors. Many people who are bullies do not realize they bully others. Once behaviors are identified, bullies can begin to change the way the act.

Materials Needed:

For the leader:

- ☐ Posterboard
- ☐ Marker
- ☐ Copy of *I Didn't Know I Was A Bully* (pages 11-32)
- ☐ Transparencies and overhead projector (optional)

For each student:

- ☐ Folder to hold worksheets for future reference and supplementary activity sheets
- ☐ Copy of *I Didn't Know I Was A Bully* (optional, pages 11-32)
- ☐ Copy of *Behavior Reflections* (page 38)
- ☐ Copy of selected supplementary activity sheets (optional, pages 95-110)
- ☐ Pencil
- ☐ Crayons or markers

Pre-Presentation Requirement:

Make a copy of *Behavior Reflections,* each chosen supplementary activity sheet, and *I Didn't Know I Was A Bully* (if being used) for each student.

Reproduce *I Didn't Know I Was A Bully* for the leader.

Using the marker, label the posterboard *Bullying Behavior List.*

Lesson:

Introduce the lesson by saying:

💬 *Today we are going to talk about* **bullying.** *Raise your hand if you are a bully.* (Allow time for the students to respond. Someone who raises his/her hand is probably trying to act silly and get attention. Acknowledge the person and ask what kind of bullying he/she does.)

Bullying is a bigger problem than most people realize. Let's take a few minutes to discuss bullying behaviors. Tell me what you think a person may do that makes him or her a bully. I will write your answers on our **Bullying Behavior List.**

Write the students' suggestions on the posterboard. Then say:

💬 *Most of the behaviors we listed are* **stereotypical** *bullying behaviors.* **Stereotypical** *refers to things we generally think of when we hear the word* **bully.** *In the next several weeks, we are going to learn about many more bullying behaviors that occur every day. We will learn that more of us are bullies than we might realize and we will learn how to change our bullying behaviors. People who are not bullies have lots of friends who truly care about them. They are fun to be around. Let's listen to a story that will help us understand what behaviors are not stereotypical bullying behaviors.*

Present *I Didn't Know I Was A Bully* to the students in one of the following ways:

1. Distribute a copy of *I Didn't Know I Was A Bully* to each student. Ask for volunteers to read one or two lines aloud. Select those students who volunteer and assign them their lines.

2. Read *I Didn't Know I Was A Bully* aloud to the students.

3. Distribute pages of *I Didn't Know I Was A Bully* to selected students and have each of them read one page. After collecting the pages, you may post them around the classroom or on a bulletin board as reminders. (You could also color the pictures to make them more visually appealing.)

4. Make transparencies of *I Didn't Know I Was A Bully*. Present the story using an overhead projector.

After *I Didn't Know I Was A Bully* has been read, ask:

> 💬 ***What additional behaviors can we add to our Bullying Behavior List?*** (Accept any appropriate answers and add the students' suggestions to list.)

Continue the discussion by saying:

> 💬 ***Now that we know what a bully does, raise your hand if you think you have been a bully or are now a bully.*** (Praise the students for being honest. Raise your hand and acknowledge that you have been a bully in the past.)
>
> ***No one is proud to admit that he or she is a bully. In fact, most people are embarrassed to think of themselves as bullies. Raise your hand if you would be embarrassed for others to think of YOU as a bully.*** (Pause for students to respond.)
>
> ***The first step in changing a behavior we don't like is to identify the behavior and understand why we act that way. We have just listed bullying behaviors. Now that we know what a bully does, we can work on changing the behavior. For the next several weeks, we will focus on specific bullying behaviors that happen to us every day. These behaviors make us sad, lonely, and hurt.***

Distribute *Behavior Reflections* and a pencil to each student. Then say:

> 💬 ***We are going to take some time to reflect or think about our own behaviors. If you are completely honest, you may identify some ways you may have bullied others in the past or ways you bully others now. Taking the time to acknowledge these behaviors is the first step in changing the way you treat others. It will make you feel much better about yourself.***
>
> ***No one is proud to call him or herself a bully. You can change your behavior. Please complete the Behavior Reflection paper as honestly as you can. I will not collect these papers, and you will not have to share anything you do not feel comfortable sharing.***

Note: To make the students feel more comfortable, describe a time that you bullied another person and how you feel about your bullying behavior.

Have the students complete their *Behavior Reflection* papers and allow those students who wish to do so to participate in a class discussion.

Distribute any supplementary activity sheets you have decided to use and crayons or markers to the students. Have the students complete and discuss the activity sheets.

Conclusion:

Distribute a folder and crayons or markers to each student. Explain that the folders are for the students to keep the papers they completed during this class. Allow time for the students to decorate their folders. Have the students place their papers in their folders. Collect the folders.

Compliment the students for identifying bullying behaviors and remind them that acknowledging any behavior is the first step in changing it.

Save the *Bullying Behavior List* for use in future sessions.

BEHAVIOR REFLECTIONS

1. List bullying behaviors you have exhibited in the past.
   _____
   _____

2. What bullying behaviors do you currently practice?
   _____
   _____

3. How do you feel about these behaviors?
   _____
   _____

4. How will you change these behaviors?
   _____
   _____

5. What will your friends see you doing differently?
   _____
   _____

6. How will your friends feel about these changes in your behavior?
   _____
   _____

7. How will you feel about these changes in your behavior?
   _____
   _____

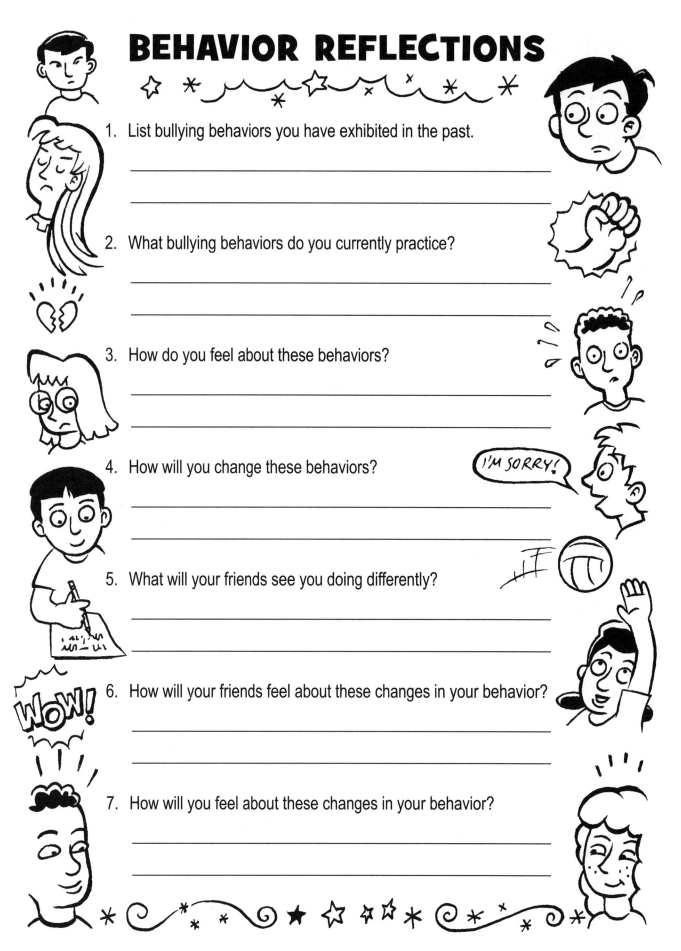

LESSON 2
BULLYING

Objective:

To help children understand how excluding others is a bullying behavior, how others feel when we exclude them, and how we can change our bullying behavior.

Materials Needed:

For the leader:

- ☐ *Bullying Behavior List* poster (from previous lesson)
- ☐ Copy of *In The Show* (page 43)
- ☐ Copy of *Choosing Sides* (page 44)
- ☐ Chalkboard and chalk

For each student:

- ☐ Student's folder (optional)
- ☐ Crayons or markers, if supplementary activity sheets are being used
- ☐ Copy of selected supplementary activity sheets (optional, pages 95-110)

Pre-Presentation Requirement:

Make a copy of each chosen supplementary activity sheet for each student.

Make a copy of *In The Show* and *Choosing Sides* for the leader.

Lesson:

Introduce the lesson by saying:

> 💬 *We began last time by discussing bullying behaviors. We learned that bullies are not just the kids who steal your lunch money and beat people up. Bullies are around us every day. We learned that WE might even be bullies. Let's review our list of bullying behaviors.*

I DIDN'T KNOW I WAS A BULLY © 2006 MAR✶CO PRODUCTS, INC. 1-800-448-2197

Have students read the *Bullying Behavior List* that was compiled during the last lesson. Then say:

> 💬 *Once we recognized our bullying behaviors, many of us admitted to being bullies at times. Remember that we said that the first step in changing a behavior is to identify and understand the behavior. Once we identify and understand the behavior, we can work to change it.*
>
> *Today we are going to concentrate on one common type of bullying behavior. This behavior is called* excluding*. Raise your hand if you know what* excluding *means.*

Call on those students with raised hands to describe *excluding* behavior. Then say:

> 💬 **Excluding** *means* **leaving others out on purpose** *in order to show power over them. I'm going to read you a story about a girl who was excluding others and being a bully. She didn't even realize she was being a bully.*

Read *In The Show* (page 43). Then discuss the following questions with the students:

1. *How would most of Sara's classmates describe her at the beginning of the story?* (Sara was confident, popular, bossy, dramatic, and any other appropriate answer.)

2. *How did Sara feel about herself before she went to drama camp?* (She felt confident, proud, popular, smart, talented, and any other appropriate answer.)

3. *What bullying behaviors did Sara use?* (Sara was excluding and bossy.)

4. *What happened at drama camp that changed Sara's feelings about herself?* (Sara was excluded from the group.)

5. *What did Sara learn about excluding others?* (Sara learned that it doesn't feel good to be excluded and left out. She also learned that she was bullying when she excluded others. She learned how to be a better friend.)

Continue the lesson by saying:

> 💬 *You have heard about one situation that involved exclusion. Now let's listen to another story about excluding others.*

Read *Choosing Sides* (page 44). Then discuss the following questions with the students:

1. ***How would Corey describe himself at the beginning of the story?*** (Corey was confident, popular, athletic, and any other appropriate answer.)

2. ***How would Corey describe himself at the end of the story?*** (He was bossy, unkind, embarrassed by his behaviors, less confident, and any other appropriate answer.) ***What caused him to change his mind?*** (He saw the look of embarrassment on the other boy's face.)

3. ***What do you think Corey will do differently?*** (Accept any appropriate answers.)

4. ***What do Sara and Corey have to do in order to change their bullying behaviors?*** (They need to realize that excluding others is a form of bullying and stop acting that way.)

Write the following discussion topics on the board.

1. Describe a time when you were excluded from a group or were left out of an activity. Describe how you felt.

2. Describe a time you excluded someone from a group or an activity. Describe how you think that person felt.

Involve the children in the following activity. Explain the activity by saying:

> ***We are going to do a partner-share activity. Choose a person to be your partner. You may not choose a person you have played with in the last two weeks. Choose someone you don't know well. Look at the sentences on the board. For the next ten minutes, you are to discuss these topics with your partner. When sharing with your partner, don't use real names. Use fake names to prevent others' feelings from being hurt. Begin by discussing the first topic. After five minutes, I will call*** time. ***You should then switch to the second topic.***

Have the children choose their partners, then tell them to begin. After five minutes, have them change topics. End the discussion after ten minutes. Then say:

> ***Based on the stories you heard and discussed and the partner-share activity, what have you learned about how people feel when we exclude them or leave them out?*** (Accept any appropriate answers.)

Continue the lesson by saying:

> 💬 *In general, we may make them feel hurt, unwanted, lonely, disappointed, embarrassed, sad, and/or angry. We cause many unpleasant feelings when we exclude others.*
>
> *There are times when a limited number of people can participate in an activity. How can we handle this without causing others to feel excluded?* (Taking turns, sharing, and forming additional teams are some of the ways this can be handled.)
>
> *We must also watch the way we talk to others. Sometimes our tone of voice or the look on our face can send unpleasant messages. These messages can cause others to feel excluded or unwanted.* (Give an example by using a harsh tone of voice while saying, "You can't sit here." Then in a normal tone of voice say, "You can't sit here because I already promised Gina I would sit by her today. I'll sit by you next time." Demonstrate sending a negative message with eye-rolling while saying, "That's not the answer." Then without eye-rolling, say, "That's not the answer. Let me show you how to do that problem.")
>
> *Being aware of what you say to others and how you say it can keep you from being a bully.*

Distribute any supplementary activity sheets you have decided to use and crayons or markers to the students. Have the students complete and discuss the activity sheets.

Conclusion:

If supplementary activity sheets were used, distribute the students' folders and have them place their activity sheets in the folders. Collect the folders.

Compliment the students for recognizing that *excluding others* is a form of *bullying*.

IN THE SHOW

Sara liked to play tag and jump rope, but most of all, she loved creating characters and directing others in her plays at recess. Sara was very good at this because she had a wonderful imagination. She dreamed up stories about fairies, princesses, dragons, and warriors. She would direct her friends in these fantastic and exciting creations. Children loved to be part of her productions.

However, Sara was very selective about who could take part in her plays. Usually, Sara let only her closest friends take part in her plays. She sometimes got quite caught up in the power she had and hurt many feelings by leaving people out or *excluding* them. Many children would ask if they could join in, but Sara turned them away. She even told some children that they were not talented enough to take part in *her* elaborate productions. These children walked away feeling sad, lonely, disappointed, and unwanted. Sara had no idea she was making them feel so bad.

One summer, Sara's parents enrolled her in a drama camp in a nearby city. Sara was very excited about going to this camp and showing off all of her wonderful dramatic talents. When she arrived, she was shocked to see so many new faces. There seemed to be hundreds of kids! Everyone was assigned to groups and drama projects. Sara didn't know any of the people in her group, but she was eager to show them all *her* wonderful talents.

As soon as the team began working on its project, Sara spoke up and began sharing her ideas. She was bursting with excitement about the project and couldn't wait for the others to hear her plan. Sara told the group her thoughts. To her surprise no one said, "That's a great idea!" No one reacted to her thoughts like she thought they would. In fact, they immediately rejected her plans. Some other children began sharing their ideas, and everyone else in the group thought *those* ideas were wonderful.

When the group began designing the project without Sara's involvement, she was shocked. It was the first time she hadn't been in charge, the first time she couldn't pick who would play certain parts, and the first time everyone didn't agree that her plans were the best. She couldn't believe what was happening! The group seemed to have no interest in Sara or her ideas.

Sara sat apart from the group and watched the planning and the fun the others were having. Sara felt totally left out, unimportant, and rejected. As Sara sat watching the group, she thought about how *her* friends would love her ideas. But then she began to think about the rest of her classmates. She wondered if those who didn't get to be part of her productions ever felt like she was feeling at that moment. Was it possible she had made them feel like she was feeling? She began to wish she had never told them they weren't talented enough to be part of her plays. She had never meant to hurt anyone. Sara now realized how she made others feel, and she felt terrible.

Sara now knew how it felt to be excluded. Over and over in her mind she kept saying, "I never knew I was a bully." Those were words she definitely did not like. She knew that she needed to change her behavior toward others.

CHOOSING SIDES

Ten more minutes. Just ten more minutes until recess. Corey had waited for this time all day. He had listened to the teacher talk about the history of their state. He had completed his spelling worksheet and had taken his test on long division. In just a few minutes, it would be time. Time to show his moves on the court.

Every day at recess, Corey and his friends played basketball. There was only one basketball court and all the fifth graders knew who got to play on it. The teacher finally told the students to line up for recess. Corey was first in line. He was ready to burst with energy. As soon as the door opened, he was out like a flash. He had the ball in his hands and was ready to choose teams.

Corey almost always got to be captain of a team and was the first to choose a player. As he checked out the kids who wanted to be on teams, he noticed the new boy from the other class. Corey laughed out loud, then said, "Hey, loser, I don't think so. Go find some other losers to play with." His remark made the other kids laugh. Corey felt pretty good until he saw the look of embarrassment on the boy's face. Cory acted like what he had said didn't bother him, but it did. He had seen kids make fun of other kids and he knew everyone thought *those* kids were bullies. All he could think of during the game was, "I never knew I was a bully." What he had done bothered him so much that those basketball moves he couldn't wait to show off never came into play. He played the worst game he had ever played. When the teacher blew the whistle for the students to line up, Corey passed the new boy, but didn't have the nerve to look him in the eye.

LESSON 3
BULLYING

Objective:

To help children understand how friends can bully one another and why "friendship power" must be equal.

Materials Needed:

For the leader:

- ☐ *Bullying Behavior List* poster (from previous lesson)
- ☐ Copy of *It's Just Funny* (pages 50)
- ☐ Copy of *Friendship Fears* (pages 51-52)
- ☐ Marker

For each student:

- ☐ Student's folder (optional)
- ☐ Crayons or markers, if supplementary activity sheets are being used
- ☐ Copy of selected supplementary activity sheets (optional, pages 95-110)

Pre-Presentation Requirement:

Make a copy of each chosen supplementary activity sheet for each student.

Make a copy of *It's Just Funny* and *Friendship Fears* for the leader.

Lesson:

Introduce the lesson by saying:

> 💬 **We have been discussing bullying behaviors. Who can tell us some examples of bullying behaviors?** (Accept all appropriate answers.)

After the students have named bullying behaviors, use the *Bullying Behavior List* to name any that have not been mentioned. Then say:

> 💬 *In our previous lessons, we have learned that most people would not like to be considered bullies. We have also learned that realizing what bullying behaviors are and admitting that you use them is the best way to change these behaviors. And in our last lesson, we discussed excluding others and how this is a form of bullying.*
>
> *Today we are going to learn about* **friendship bullies.** *You are probably wondering to yourself, "How do friends bully?" Actually, friends do quite a bit of bullying at times. How do you think friends might bully one another?* (Accept appropriate answers and add them to the *Bully Behavior List*.)

If the following behaviors are not mentioned, bring them to the students' attention and add them to the *Bully Behavior List*.

- Friends sometimes say things like:
    - "I'm not going to be your friend if…"
    - "I'll be your friend if…"
- Friends sometimes call each other names.
- Friends sometimes boss each other.
- Friends sometimes tease and laugh at one another.
- Friends sometimes pout and cry when they don't get their way.

Continue the lesson by saying:

> 💬 *We often bully our friends and don't even realize we are doing it. We are putting them down or hurting their feelings, and they are too embarrassed or too scared to tell us. They worry that we will stop being their friend. Friends should not have such power over each other. "Friendship power" should be equal.*
>
> *I would like you to listen to this story about two boys who were dealing with unequal "friendship power." That is another name for bullying.*

Read *It's Just Funny* (page 50). Then discuss the following questions with the students:

1. **How did Jarod feel about Alex's name-calling at the beginning of the story?** (He knew it was wrong and that it was a bad habit, but he ignored it because it didn't affect him, yet.)

2. ***How did Jarod feel about Alex's name-calling by the end of the story?*** (He didn't like it. He felt angry, upset, embarrassed, and bullied.)

3. ***What could Jarod do about this friendship bullying?*** (Jarod could confront Alex by telling him how he feels when he is called names and ask Alex to stop. If that doesn't work, Jarod could ask for help from an adult.)

Then say to the students:

💬 ***Most people do not want to be called names. Some people like to be called by a nickname. You should call someone by a nickname only if he or she has asked you to do so.***

Sometimes friends allow themselves to be bullied because they worry about losing a friendship. What they don't realize is that continued friendship bullying causes them to end up losing their friend anyway. I want you to think about the next question I am going to ask. Answer it to yourself. Do you treat your friends the way you want to be treated? (Pause for students to answer the question to themselves.) ***If you do not, you may be bullying your friends.***

Listen to this story of typical friendship bullying.

Read *Friendship Fears* (pages 51-52). Then discuss the following questions with the students:

1. ***What bullying behaviors were described in this story?*** (The bullying behaviors were bossing, controlling, unequal friendship power, threats, and any other appropriate answers.)

2. ***How could these behaviors change a friendship?*** (They could cause a friendship to become very uncomfortable and even end.)

3. ***What could Jessica do to deal with this friendship bullying?*** (Jessica could confront Kaya and tell her how she feels about Kaya's behavior. She could also help Kaya and Rachel get to know one another better. If these attempts did not work, Jessica could ask for help from an adult.)

Explain to the students:

💬 ***Friendships are not always easy. They all have bumps and hard times and it takes work to make them last. Friends should have equal power in the relation-***

ship. A true friendship is not one in which one person controls the other person. When this occurs, it is bullying. This is not fair. When a friend tries to control you, it's okay to remind your friend that YOU control yourself. When a person behaves in a way that is upsetting to you, you can tell that person how you feel and what you would like him or her to do. This is called an **I Message**. *Using an* **I Message** *is a good way to equalize the power in a relationship. When you use an* **I Message**, *you stand up to your friend without running the risk of losing the friendship. If using an* **I Message** *does not work, ask an adult for help in talking out the problem.*

Here are some examples of friendship I Messages:

1. *I feel angry when you tell me whom I can play with at recess. I want you to please stop bossing me around.*

2. *I feel annoyed when you call me that name. I want you to please call me by my real name.*

3. *I feel embarrassed when you laugh at me in math class for giving the wrong answer. I want you to please stop.*

Have the students perform a few role-plays demonstrating friendship bullying and ways to deal with it. Choose students to be the bully and the victim. Remind the victim that he/she can stand up to the bully without losing his/her friendship.

Role-Plays:

1. Caleb threatens to tell Ryan's secret about a girl Ryan thinks is cute if he doesn't play the game Caleb wants to play at recess.

2. Maria tells Jodie that she must sit by her at lunch instead of beside Allison.

3. Ben tells Adam what to play every day at recess. Adam never gets to choose the activity or game.

4. Miranda pouts and cries when Shanna and Pamela don't let her have her way.

Distribute any supplementary activity sheets you have decided to use and crayons or markers to the students. Have the students complete and discuss the activity sheets.

Conclusion:

If supplementary activity sheets were used, distribute the students' folders and have them place their activity sheets in the folders. Collect the folders.

Tell the students:

> 💬 *Remember: "Friendship power" should be equal. You do not have the right to control other people and others should not have power over you.*

IT'S JUST FUNNY

Jarod and Alex were good friends. They were in the same grade and hung out with the same group of guys every day. They did lots of things together and even spent lots of time together at home. They were always at each other's houses on weekends and in the summer. There was only one problem. Alex could be a little bossy and had a bad habit of calling people names.

Alex had invited Jarod to spend the weekend at his house and go to a theme park. On Saturday morning, Jarod's mom dropped him off at Alex's house. Jarod was really excited, because he loved to ride roller coasters. Shortly after he arrived, Jarod began feeling sick to his stomach. He tried to ignore the feeling, because he didn't want anything to ruin the day. Unfortunately, Jarod began feeling worse and even vomited. Knowing that the theme park wouldn't be a good place for a sick boy, Alex's parents called Jarod's mom to come and pick him up. Jarod felt sick to his stomach and extremely upset. Alex was disappointed, too, but decided to invite Thomas to go with him. After all, it's no fun to ride roller coasters all alone.

When Alex saw Jarod at school on Monday, he called his friend *barf-boy*. Alex then told Jarod about all the fun he and Thomas had at the park. Jarod felt jealous that Thomas had gone in his place, but he was more upset that Alex was rubbing it in by calling him *barf-boy*. He knew that Alex had a habit of giving people nicknames that were unkind. Usually others were the recipients of the teasing, and Jarod just hoped his new nickname would not stick.

Much to Jarod's dismay, Alex continued to call him *barf-boy*. Alex thought it was funny. So did the rest of the gang. The next morning, Alex saw Jarod get off the bus and yelled, "Good morning, *barf-boy*. Jarod didn't even look up at him. Alex thought it was strange that Jarod didn't seem to notice that he was talking to him. Once they got into the classroom, Alex whispered, "Hey, *barf-boy*, do you want to play basketball at recess?" Jarod still did not look at Alex or answer him. At recess, Jarod didn't join Alex and the others at the court. He played tetherball with kids from the other class. Alex could not understand why Jarod was acting that way. He *always* hung out with the group. This went on for the rest of the week. Alex tried to make Jarod laugh by teasing with him or calling other people funny names, but nothing worked. Jarod just ignored him and Alex couldn't imagine why Jarod didn't seem interested in being his friend any more.

FRIENDSHIP FEARS

Jessica and Kaya had been best friends since preschool. They were always in class together and played on the same sports teams. They knew all of one another's favorites, secrets, and worries. Jessica and Kaya were inseparable.

When the new school year began, the girls couldn't wait to see who their teacher was going to be. They had always been in the same class and hoped they would be this year, too. On the first day of school, they went to their grade level and looked at the class lists posted on the door of each classroom. They found Jessica's name on one classroom door, but Kaya's was not listed there. Then they went to the other classrooms and read the lists until they found Kaya's name. For the first time ever, they would be in separate rooms. Used to being together and wanting to be together, Jessica and Kaya were really disappointed. They were even a bit nervous about being in different classrooms.

When the school day began, Jessica was assigned to a seat beside a girl named Rachel. The two girls had never been in class together before. After a few days, Jessica began to really like Rachel. She liked to play the same games, read the same books, and watch the same TV shows as Jessica did. Besides, Rachel was really nice.

Jessica saw Kaya every day at recess and, as soon as they both got home from school, they were on the phone with one another. They told each other about what had happened during the day, then Jessica began telling Kaya about Rachel. Whenever Jessica mentioned Rachel, Kaya would get really quiet. She didn't like to hear about Jessica and Rachel getting along so well. All Kaya could think of was that if the two of them got along so well, she might lose Jessica to Rachel.

After a few weeks of school, Rachel invited Jessica over to her house to play. Jessica thought going would be a lot of fun. She was very excited and, because she and Kaya had always shared everything, she told Kaya about the invitation. Hearing about the invitation and Jessica's excitement to accept it made Kaya really, really angry. Thinking a threat might prevent Rachel from stealing Jessica from her as a friend, Kaya said, "If you go to Rachel's house, that is the end of our friendship. It's either her or me." And without another word, Kaya hung up the phone. Jessica was shocked! Kaya had never hung up on her before, and she certainly had never talked to her this way. At first, Jessica was hurt and sad to think that Kaya would act that way to her, then she became angry. Kaya was trying to boss her around, and the more Jessica thought about that, the angrier she became.

The next day at school, Kaya began giving Jessica dirty looks and making mean faces. Jessica was really confused. She liked Rachel and wanted to go to her house, but she didn't want to lose Kaya as a friend. Jessica didn't know what to do.

Kaya, on the other hand, felt horrible. She thought her world was falling apart. She felt angry and jealous on the inside. She, too, was worried that she was losing her best friend. She could not believe that Jessica would choose Rachel instead of her. Or would she?

LESSON 4
BULLYING

Objective:

To review bullying behaviors covered in previous lessons, to define cyberbullying, and to help children understand what to do if they witness bullying.

Materials Needed:

For the leader:

- ☐ *Bullying Behavior List* poster (from previous lesson)
- ☐ Copy of *The Cyberbully* (pages 57-58)
- ☐ Copy of *I Wasn't The Bully* (page 59)
- ☐ Marker

For each student:

- ☐ Student's folder (optional)
- ☐ Crayons or markers, if supplementary activity sheets are being used
- ☐ Copy of selected supplementary activity sheets (optional, pages 95-110)

Pre-Presentation Requirement:

Make a copy of each chosen supplementary activity sheet for each student.

Make a copy of *The Cyberbully* and *I Wasn't The Bully* for the leader.

Lesson:

Introduce the lesson by saying:

> 💬 *Let's see what we've learned in the last three lessons. If you think the answers to the following questions are true, give me a thumb's-up. Give me a thumb's-down if you think the answer is false.*

I DIDN'T KNOW I WAS A BULLY © 2006 MAR✶CO PRODUCTS, INC. 1-800-448-2197

Bullies are only people who hit others. (False)
Bullies are always strangers. (False)
Bullies can be friends. (True)
Bullies are always people who are lonely and insecure. (False)
Bullies may think they are funny. (True)
Bullies like to have all the friendship power. (True)
Bullies can change their behavior. (True)
Being a bully is cool. (False)

Continue the lesson by saying:

💬 *We've learned that bullies don't all look alike. A bully can be someone who physically harms or threatens to harm others. Bullies might be close friends who try to control and have power over others. Bullies cause victims to feel embarrassed, lonely, sad, unwanted, or even powerless. Bullies are unpleasant to be around. However, we often continue to allow them to treat us in this negative way because we fear being rejected or embarrassed even more. In our lessons, we have learned some strategies we can use in dealing with bullies. Raise your hand if you remember what you can do to deal with a bully.* (Call on students and praise answers dealing with *I Messages* and getting help from an adult.)

Today we are going to learn about some different forms of bullying. Sometimes bullies try to put others down or intimidate them by writing negative things about them. Bullies may pass notes containing rumors, lies, and threats. Bullies may start "popularity booklets" that exclude others or even put people down. Sometimes bullying can become very high-tech. This is called **cyberbullying.** *Cyberbullying occurs when computers are used to send negative messages to or about someone. This form of bullying is very hurtful to the victim and it is not wise for the bully. Listen to the story called The Cyberbully.*

Read *The Cyberbully* (pages 57-58). Then discuss the following questions with the students:

1. **What bad choices were made in the story and who made them?** (Accept any appropriate answers.)

2. **How could Michelle have handled her feelings of jealousy differently?** (She could have reminded herself that her friends care about her even when they are with other people. She could have used an *I Message* to talk about her feelings with her friends. She could have discussed her feelings with a trusted adult. She could have attempted to get to know Tori better before deciding if she liked her.)

Tell the students:

> *In the story about Michelle, we saw how someone can use the Internet to bully others. When her friends found out she had told a lie, it was obvious to everyone that Michelle was bullying. Gossip, particularly malicious gossip, is a form of bullying.*
>
> *Sometimes it is not easy to identify a bully. The story we are about to hear tells of children who support bullying without realizing it.*

Read *I Wasn't The Bully* (page 59). Then discuss the following questions with the students:

1. *What bad choices were made in the story and who made them?* (Accept any appropriate answers.)

2. *How could Jason have handled the bullying?* (He could have asked the bullies to stop or he could have gotten help from an adult.)

Then continue the lesson by saying:

> *Making up lies about others is wrong. This is a form of bullying. Putting others down on purpose is bullying. Even spreading rumors about other people contributes to bullying. You always have the choice to bully or not to bully. You always have the choice to support bullying or not support bullying. Spreading rumors, laughing at teasing or putdowns, sending negative messages in notes or on the computer, not confronting the bully, or not reporting bullying to an adult are ways of supporting bullying behavior. Bullying behavior should be pointed out for what it is. Remember: Whenever you see or are involved in a bullying situation, you have a choice. Choosing to ignore bullying behavior is the same as supporting the bully. Choosing to support bullying is always a bad choice.*
>
> *It is okay to:*
>
> - *Ask a friend to stop bullying others.*
> - *Use an I Message to ask someone to stop bullying you.*
> - *Tell an adult about bullying.*
>
> *When you do something about a bullying situation, you have chosen not to support the bullying behavior. You are letting the bully know his or her behavior is unacceptable.*

Then say:

> *Feeling jealous and worried that you might lose your friends is very normal. However, there are other ways to deal with these feelings. Talking with your friends about your worries is helpful. Everyone has these feelings from time to time. Getting to know the person you are jealous of is also helpful. You might even decide that you like that person as a friend.*

Have one or two volunteers retell *The Cyberbully*. This will refresh the students' memory of what the story was about. Then have one or two volunteers retell *I Wasn't The Bully* to refresh the students' memory of the story.

Divide the class into small groups. Assign one of the stories to each group. Tell the students to work together and decide on alternate endings. The students assigned to *The Cyberbully* should come up with endings that will help Michelle avoid bullying behavior. The students assigned to *I Wasn't The Bully* should come up with endings that will help Jason to not support the bullying behaviors of the boys on the bus. Determine the amount of time the students have to complete the task. When the allotted time has elapsed, have each group share its ending with the class.

Review the behaviors written on the *Bullying Behavior List*. Then ask the students to think about today's lesson and decide if they learned any new bullying behaviors that should be added to the list. Add the students' contributions to the poster.

Distribute any supplementary activity sheets you have decided to use and crayons or markers to the students. Have the students complete and discuss the activity sheets.

Conclusion:

If supplementary activity sheets were used, distribute the students' folders and have them place their activity sheets in the folders. Collect the folders.

Tell the students:

> *You have learned a great deal about the power of bullying, but you have also learned that you have a greater power. You have learned what behaviors are considered to be bullying, how exclusion is a form of bullying, that "friendship power" should be equal, and what techniques you can use to discourage bullying. This knowledge will make you able to better handle bullying situations involving yourself and others.*

THE CYBERBULLY

Michelle couldn't wait to get home from vacation to hear the latest news from her friends. She had been out of town with her family for a whole week, and she was anxious to hear the latest gossip. Even though she'd had a great time with her family, she had missed her friends and was curious about what had been going on.

She quickly unpacked her bags and logged onto the computer. "Instant messaging is awesome," she thought to herself. Her screen name was "Pinky," and all her classmates knew it. Pink was Michelle's favorite color, she almost always wore it. She was often called "Pinky" at school instead of Michelle.

Michelle read what seemed to be a hundred messages. She loved hearing what had happened while she was gone. That was until she read the last message. This message was from her best friend. It said that Tori, a girl in Michelle's class, had a great slumber party while Michelle was out of town. Michelle's whole group of friends had attended. Michelle didn't particularly like Tori and wasn't happy that she had hosted such an awesome party. In fact, Michelle was more than unhappy, she was furious.

Michelle would show Tori that she could not steal *her* friends!.

Michelle decided to make up a story about Tori that would make the others not want to be Tori's friend. She began typing a long lie about how she had seen Tori shoplifting in the mall. She wrote that the manager of the store had caught Tori and that she wasn't allowed in the mall any more. As she read over her tale, Michelle felt guilty but satisfied that she would keep her friends from abandoning her for Tori. She clicked the "send all" icon on her computer screen so the message would immediately go to all of her friends' computers.

After Michelle logged off the computer, her mother told her she had a message on the answering machine. Michelle went into the kitchen to listen to the message. It was Tori's voice, inviting her to the party. Tori didn't know that Michelle was out of town on vacation and said that she hoped Michelle could come to her party. Upon hearing Tori's kind words, Michelle felt like she wanted to sink into a hole, away from everyone. She couldn't take back the lie she had just sent to all of her friends.

The gang started getting the messages and everyone was shocked at what she read. Whether they believed the gossip or not, it was juicy to read. Some of the group even forwarded the message to other friends and classmates. The message quickly traveled to people across the Internet, all of whom knew the original sender was "Pinky."

The incident became worse when someone sent the message to Tori. She was devastated by the lie she read. She had not shoplifted at the mall. She began to cry out of anger and embarrassment that so many people might believe the story to be true. She quickly showed her parents the message that had been sent to countless people. They were so upset that they immediately contacted Michelle's parents.

Michelle's parents were disappointed and furious with their daughter. Michelle ended up in more trouble than she had ever been in. Once Michelle's friends learned the story was a lie, they were shocked, too. This was not the Michelle they knew and had been friends with for many years. Many of them felt they could never trust her again and weren't sure whether they wanted to remain friends with her. If she would make up lies about Tori, she might do the same to one of them.

I WASN'T THE BULLY

Jason's fourth-grade science class had studied about fish and other aquatic creatures for weeks. As a special treat at the end of the grading period, the students took a field trip to the Aquarium. There they saw fish and marine animals that they had studied about and some they had never heard of. But of all the sights they saw, the shark tank was definitely the best. Jason was particularly excited about the day. He hoped to be a marine biologist when he grew up.

Later the students had a picnic lunch in a nearby park. It had been a great day. Now it was time to head back to school on the bus.

The kids quickly lined up to board the bus. Everyone wanted to get the seats in the back, because the adults usually sat near the front. Mike and Ryan were the first ones on and they hurried to the back of the bus. Then everyone else piled onto the bus. Jason ended up sitting directly in front of Mike and Ryan. He wasn't a close friend of the two, but he didn't dislike them, either.

As the bus started heading back to school, Jason overheard two other kids making mean jokes about MIke. They were loud and were making sure Mike heard what they were saying. The two kids who were making the putdowns happened to be friends of Jason's. He had heard them say mean things before but he had never heard them say anything this bad or say anything bad loud enough for the person they were talking about to hear. The teasing and taunting continued. Mike began to get upset, and Jason felt bad for him. He wanted his friends to stop being cruel. But after all, they were his friends. If he asked them to stop, he knew they would get mad at him. He worried that they might even start being mean to him. Still, he knew what they were doing was wrong. He also knew better than to join in the bullying. He decided to just sit there and hope it would stop.

LESSON 5
BULLYING

Objective:

To review bullying behaviors previously discussed and learn strategies in changing bullying behaviors and other negative behaviors.

Materials Needed:

For the leader:

- ☐ *Bullying Behavior List* poster (from previous lesson)
- ☐ Copy of *In The Show* (pages 63-64)

For each student:

- ☐ Student's folder
- ☐ Copy of *Behavior-Change Steps* (page 65)
- ☐ Copy of *Behavior-Change Worksheet* (page 66)
- ☐ Pencil

Pre-Presentation Requirement:

Make a copy of *Behavior-Change Steps* and *Behavior-Change Worksheet* for each student.

Make a copy of *In The Show* for the leader.

Lesson:

Distribute the students' folders, then introduce the lesson by saying:

> 💬 *Today we are going to learn some strategies we can use to change bullying behaviors. We have already learned about some typical bullying behaviors. Let's review what bullying looks like.*

Call on several students to read the *Bullying Behavior List*. Then continue the lesson by saying:

> 💬 ***We now know what behaviors are bullying behaviors and that if we are doing these things, we need to change. Remember: Identifying and understanding the problem is the first step in fixing it. We must admit that what we are doing is unkind and bullying toward others.***
>
> ***We looked at those behaviors a few lessons ago when we completed the* Behavior Reflections *page. Please take this paper out of your folder to remind yourself what you identified as a concern for yourself.***

Allow time for the students to review their papers. Ask the students if they would like to share a few behaviors identified on the sheet. Acknowledge those students who do so for being brave enough to publicly acknowledge their bullying behaviors. Then say:

> 💬 ***Now that we know what behaviors we want to change or improve, we need to come up with a strategy or plan for correcting those behaviors. Raise your hand if you have an idea about how to change these behaviors.***

Allow the students to share their ideas. Accept all appropriate answers. Then say:

> 💬 ***Let's revisit one of the stories about bullying that we previously heard and see how that student changed her bullying behaviors.***

Read *In The Show* (pages 63-64). Then discuss the following questions with the students:

1. ***What did Sara do to change her behavior?*** (Sara understood what bullying behaviors were, she admitted that she had been bullying others, she talked about the problem with someone, she came up with a plan, she apologized for bullying, and she acknowledged her progress.)

2. ***How do you think this behavior change will affect Sara in the future?*** (Accept all appropriate answers.)

Distribute *Behavior-Change Steps* to each student. Have the students read the steps and discuss how Sara followed the steps in changing her behavior. Then say:

> 💬 ***These steps work not only with bullying behaviors, but with other negative behaviors we might use. Can you think of other behaviors these steps might also help to improve?*** (Accept any appropriate answers.)

Continue the lesson by saying:

> *Now let's look again at our own bullying behaviors or other negative behaviors we might want to change. Look once again at your **Behavior Reflections** page. See if you could use these steps to change those behaviors. I will give you a minute to think about this. During that time, I will pass out the **Behavior-Change Worksheet** that you can use to start writing a plan.*

Distribute the *Behavior Change Worksheet* and a pencil to each student and tell the students how much time is left for them to work on it.

Conclusion:

When the allotted time has elapsed, have those students who wish to do so share their plans with the class. Then tell the students:

> *Just like Sara worked through the steps to change her behavior, you can change your behaviors. Changing behavior doesn't happen overnight. It takes time and effort. If you truly want to change, you can do it. You may need help, though. It's okay to ask a trusted adult or friend to help you with this. No one is perfect. We can all improve our relationships with others. These behavior-change strategies are steps you can use for the rest of your life.*

Have the students place their papers in their folders. Collect the folders.

IN THE SHOW

Sara liked to play tag and jump rope, but most of all, she loved creating characters and directing others in her plays at recess. Sara was very good at this because she had a wonderful imagination. She dreamed up stories about fairies, princesses, dragons, and warriors. She would direct her friends in these fantastic and exciting creations. Children loved to be part of her productions.

However, Sara was very selective about who could take part in her plays. Usually, Sara let only her closest friends take part in her plays. She sometimes got quite caught up in the power she had and hurt many feelings by leaving people out or *excluding* them. Many children would ask if they could join in, but Sara turned them away. She even told some children that they were not talented enough to take part in *her* elaborate productions. These children walked away feeling sad, lonely, disappointed, and unwanted. Sara had no idea she was making them feel so bad.

One summer, Sara's parents enrolled her in a drama camp in a nearby city. Sara was very excited about going to this camp and showing off all of her wonderful dramatic talents. When she arrived, she was shocked to see so many new faces. There seemed to be hundreds of kids! Everyone was assigned to groups and drama projects. Sara didn't know any of the people in her group, but she was eager to show them all *her* wonderful talents.

As soon as the team began working on its project, Sara spoke up and began sharing her ideas. She was bursting with excitement about the project and couldn't wait for the others to hear her plan. Sara told the group her thoughts. To her surprise no one said, "That's a great idea!" No one reacted to her thoughts like she thought they would. In fact, they immediately rejected her plans. Some other children began sharing their ideas, and everyone else in the group thought *those* ideas were wonderful.

When the group began designing the project without Sara's involvement, she was shocked. It was the first time she hadn't been in charge, the first time she couldn't pick who would play certain parts, and the first time everyone didn't agree that her plans were the best. She couldn't believe what was happening! The group seemed to have no interest in Sara or her ideas.

Sara sat apart from the group and watched the planning and the fun the others were having. Sara felt totally left out, unimportant, and rejected. As Sara sat watching the group, she thought about how *her* friends would love her ideas. But then she began to think about the rest of her classmates. She wondered if those who didn't get to be part of her productions ever felt like she was feeling at that moment. Was it possible she had made them feel like she was feeling? She began to wish she had never told them they weren't talented enough to be part of her plays. She had never meant to hurt anyone. Sara now realized how she made others feel, and she felt terrible.

Sara now knew how it felt to be excluded. Over and over in her mind she kept saying, "I never knew I was a bully." Those were words she definitely did not like. She knew that she needed to change her behavior toward others.

When Sara arrived home from camp, she told her mother all about what had happened. She told her about the kids not wanting to include her ideas and how she felt left out. She was also very honest about how she had sometimes treated the other kids at school. She was feeling very ashamed of her behavior toward her classmates.

Mother listened carefully. When Sara was finished speaking, Sara's mother told her that recognizing faults was the first step toward changing behavior and that she was very proud of Sara for being able to do this. Sara felt very relieved to discuss this with someone. She decided to immediately make an effort to change her behavior. She asked her mom to help her with the plan. First, Sara made a poster for her room that reminded her every morning what kind of friend she wanted to be to everyone. As she dressed for school, she would read the poster and focus on the person she wanted to be.

When she arrived at school, she tried her best to include others and have a positive and friendly attitude. She even apologized to the people she had excluded. This was not easy, but Sara knew it was the right thing to do. There were times when she forgot her new plan, but she tried to be patient and treat others the way she wanted to be treated.

Every day Sara gave her mom an update on how things were going at school. She and her mom noticed that Sara was making lots more friends. The music teacher even asked her to assist in directing the Spring Pageant. Her teacher noticed the change in Sara and how well she was getting along with everyone. But most important of all, Sara felt very good about her actions at the end of every day. She had tackled a big problem in herself, and the rewards were plentiful.

BEHAVIOR-CHANGE STEPS

Step 1: Understand and identify behavior that is negative or unacceptable.

Step 2: Acknowledge that you need to change the negative or unacceptable behavior.

Step 3: Come up with a strategy to change the behavior.

- Write a plan to improve the behavior.
- Talk about the behavior with someone you trust.
- Imagine yourself showing the improved behavior.
- Remind yourself regularly about the improved behavior.
- Report your progress to someone regularly.
- Keep a journal to record your progress.
- Don't give up when you make a mistake.

Step 4: Apologize or make amends for negative behavior.

Step 5: Praise yourself for any positive behavior change.

BEHAVIOR-CHANGE WORKSHEET

Step 1: What behaviors have you found to be negative and unacceptable?
_____
_____

Step 2: What behaviors do you feel you need to change?
_____
_____

Step 3: What can you do to change these behaviors?

_____ Write a plan to change negative or unacceptable behavior.
_____ Talk about the behavior with someone I trust.
_____ Imagine myself showing improved behavior.
_____ Remind myself regularly about the improved behavior.
_____ Report to someone about my progress.
_____ Keep a journal to record my progress.
_____ Don't give up when I make a mistake.
_____ Other strategies:
_____
_____

Step 4: Whom should I apologize to for my negative behavior?
_____

Step 5: How could I reward or praise myself for behavior changes?
_____
_____

LESSON 6
BULLYING

Objective:

To review the problems of bullying and help children further understand how bullying affects others. To reinforce the need for changing negative behavior and the positive benefits of behavior change and growth. (This will be achieved through bullying centers where students will work cooperatively with partners.)

Materials Needed:

For the leader:

- ☐ Library books dealing with bullying
- ☐ Materials for the selected bullying centers (pages 69-93)

For each student:

- ☐ Student's folder

Pre-Presentation Requirement:

Determine the number of pairs of students in the class and prepare that number of centers. Most of the centers may be duplicated, so duplicating eight different centers would yield a total of 16 centers accommodating 32 students. Choose supplementary activities and library books for the students to utilize during center time.

Center Suggestions:

- Play the *Bob The Bully* card game. This game requires reproducing the cards (pages 70-74) for each center.
- Design a *Bullying* bulletin board.
- Read a book about bullying.
- Search the Web for *bullying* (if computers are available).

- Play *Bullying Behavior Tic Tac Toe*. This game requires reproducing the *Question Cards* (pages 83-85) for each center.
- Do the *Bullying Word Search.*
- Do the *Bullying Crossword Puzzle.*
- Create filmstrips about bullying.

Reproduce the instructions for each center and gather the materials needed. Set up the centers in the classroom. Determine how long you will allow the pairs of students to work on one center. At the end of the allotted time or upon completion of the activity, ask the pairs of students to try other centers. These activities could be carried on over several days.

Lesson:

Distribute the students' folders. Then introduce the lesson by telling the students:

> *Today we are going to enjoy some activities to help remind us what we have learned about bullying. We will be working in pairs at centers. Many of you probably worked in centers in younger grades. You will choose a partner you have not played with in the past several weeks and work through some of the centers together. Some centers are games, some are activities, some may involve reading about bullying or allow you to research bullying on the computer. I will expect you to work cooperatively with your partner, WITHOUT BEING A BULLY. When you have completed an activity or when time is up, I will ask you to move to another center. Are there any questions?*

Have the students form pairs. Show them the center choices. Show them where they will be working and what materials they may need.

Conclusion:

Have each student orally complete the following sentence.

> One thing I learned in this class about bullying is _____.

Thank the students for their participation and tell them they may take their folders home.

BOB THE BULLY CARD GAME CENTER INSTRUCTIONS

(Played Like *Old Maid*)

You will find copies of the *Bob The Bully Cards* at your center.

Here's what you are to do:

1. Choose a dealer. The dealer will shuffle the cards and deal all of them.

2. Look at your cards to find matching pairs. Lay down all matching pairs.

3. Begin taking turns taking a card from your partner's hand. If the card you choose matches your card, lay both cards down.

4. After all of the cards have been matched, the player without the *Bob The Bully* card is the winner.

JOYFUL JAN	HELPING HANNAH	HELPING HANNAH

BOB THE BULLY CARD GAME © 2006 MAR*CO PRODUCTS, INC.	BOB THE BULLY CARD GAME © 2006 MAR*CO PRODUCTS, INC.	BOB THE BULLY CARD GAME © 2006 MAR*CO PRODUCTS, INC.
TRUSTWORTHY THOMAS	TRUSTWORTHY THOMAS	INCLUDING IDA

BOB THE BULLY CARD GAME © 2006 MAR*CO PRODUCTS, INC.	BOB THE BULLY CARD GAME © 2006 MAR*CO PRODUCTS, INC.	BOB THE BULLY CARD GAME © 2006 MAR*CO PRODUCTS, INC.
INCLUDING IDA	PEACEFUL PAM	PEACEFUL PAM

BOB THE BULLY CARD GAME © 2006 MAR*CO PRODUCTS, INC.	BOB THE BULLY CARD GAME © 2006 MAR*CO PRODUCTS, INC.	BOB THE BULLY CARD GAME © 2006 MAR*CO PRODUCTS, INC.

I DIDN'T KNOW I WAS A BULLY © 2006 MAR*CO PRODUCTS, INC. 1-800-448-2197

BULLYING BULLETIN BOARD CENTER INSTRUCTIONS

You will find copies of the *Bullying Bulletin Board*, pencils, crayons, and markers at your center.

Here's what you are to do:

1. With your partner, design a bulletin board that will show how not to be a bully or what to do if you are being bullied.

2. Your bulletin board can feature:

    Types of Bullies
    How to Deal with Bullies
    How to Change Bullying Behaviors

3. Be creative. Don't forget to add color!

4. When you have finished, put your design into your folder or your partner's folder.

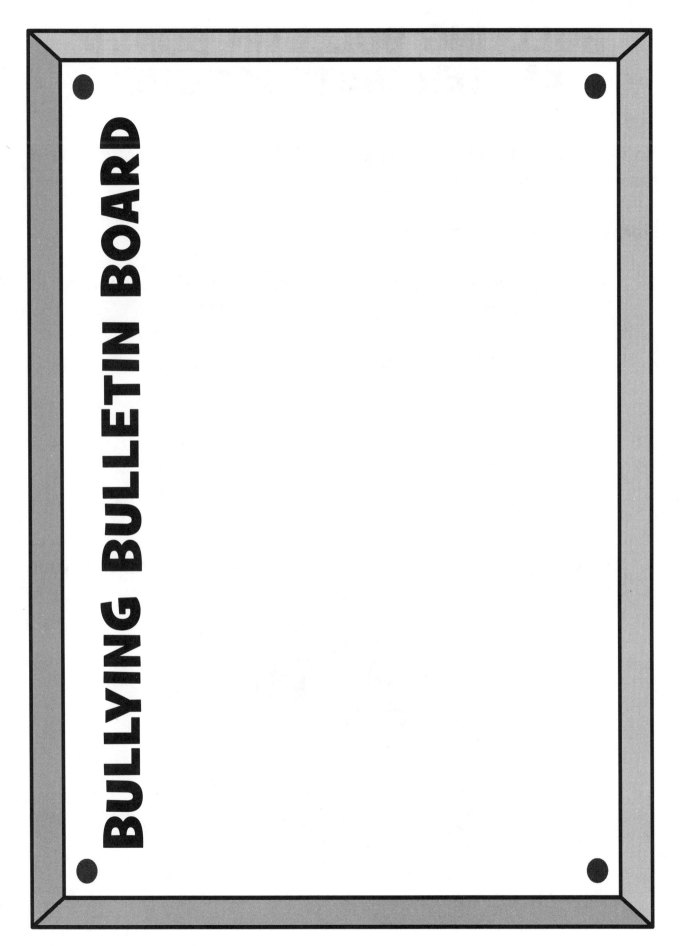

BULLYING BOOK CENTER INSTRUCTIONS

You will find books about bullying, copies of the *Bullying Book Reading Activity,* and pencils at your center.

Here's what you are to do:

1. With your partner, select a book you would both like to read.

2. After reading the story about bullying, each of you should complete the *Bullying Book Reading Activity.* Do not work together when completing the sheet.

3. When you have finished, discuss your answers with your partner.

4. When you have finished discussing your answers with your partner, put your activity sheets into your folders.

BULLYING BOOK READING ACTIVITY

Title of the book you read on bullying: _____

Who was the author? _____

Who were the characters in the story?

_____

_____

How did the story involve bullying?

_____

_____

_____

What kind of bullying was mentioned in the story? _____

Did the characters handle the bullying well? Explain why.

_____

_____

Would you have handled the bullying differently? _____

If so, what would you have done?

_____

_____

_____

78   *I DIDN'T KNOW I WAS A BULLY* © 2006 MAR*CO PRODUCTS, INC. 1-800-448-2197

BULLYING WEB SEARCH CENTER INSTRUCTIONS

You will find copies of the *Bullying Web Search* and pencils at your center.

Here's what you are to do:

1. With your partner, log onto the Internet. Type in **bullying** to search for information, games, surveys, etc. on the topic.

2. After investigating the topic, each partner should complete the *Bullying Web Search* activity sheet. Do not work with your partner while completing the activity sheet.

3. When you have both completed the activity sheet, discuss your findings with your partner.

4. When you have finished discussing your findings with your partner, put your activity sheets into your folders.

BULLYING WEB SEARCH

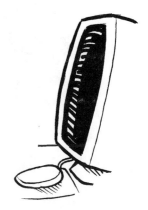

Type *bullying* into the Internet search engine.

List the sites you found:

What did you learn from the Web search?

What information or ideas could you share with others?

BULLYING BEHAVIOR TIC-TAC-TOE CENTER INSTRUCTIONS

You will find copies of the *Bullying Behavior Tic-Tac-Toe Boards,* question cards in a sealed bag, and pencils at your center.

Here's what you are to do:

1. You and your partner will decide which of you will be the first player. That player will take the question cards from the sealed bag, shuffle them, and stack them question-side down.

2. The first player will then draw a card, read the question, and answer it.

3. If both players agree the answer is correct, the player who drew the card will place an "X" or "O" on the Tic-Tac-Toe board. The other partner then takes a turn. If the players do not agree or are not sure the answer is correct, they should raise their hands and have the teacher determine which answer is correct.

4. The first player to get Tic-Tac-Toe wins. Play six games.

5. When you have finished all six games, put your activity sheets into your folders.

BULLYING BEHAVIOR TIC-TAC-TOE

BULLYING BEHAVIOR TIC-TAC-TOE

BULLYING BEHAVIOR TIC-TAC-TOE

BULLYING BEHAVIOR TIC-TAC-TOE

BULLYING BEHAVIOR TIC-TAC-TOE

BULLYING BEHAVIOR TIC-TAC-TOE

Sarah tells Joan whom she can sit with at lunch. Is Sarah a bully? Yes or No ――――――――――――――― *BULLYING BEHAVIOR TIC-TAC-TOE CARDS* © 2006 MAR*CO PRODUCTS, INC. 1-800-448-2197	John sent computer messages to Mary saying that Tom cheated on a test. Is John cyberbullying? Yes or No ――――――――――――――― *BULLYING BEHAVIOR TIC-TAC-TOE CARDS* © 2006 MAR*CO PRODUCTS, INC. 1-800-448-2197
Sue rolled her eyes at Kendra when she walked into the room. Did Sue bully Kendra? Yes or No ――――――――――――――― *BULLYING BEHAVIOR TIC-TAC-TOE CARDS* © 2006 MAR*CO PRODUCTS, INC. 1-800-448-2197	Tanya asked Kelli to join the game at recess. Did Tanya bully Kelli? Yes or No ――――――――――――――― *BULLYING BEHAVIOR TIC-TAC-TOE CARDS* © 2006 MAR*CO PRODUCTS, INC. 1-800-448-2197
Jill told Kim that she could invite Tara over to swim at her house, too. Did Jill bully Kim? Yes or No ――――――――――――――― *BULLYING BEHAVIOR TIC-TAC-TOE CARDS* © 2006 MAR*CO PRODUCTS, INC. 1-800-448-2197	Martin called Tom a "freak." Did Martin bully Tom? Yes or No ――――――――――――――― *BULLYING BEHAVIOR TIC-TAC-TOE CARDS* © 2006 MAR*CO PRODUCTS, INC. 1-800-448-2197
McKenzie told Josie she wasn't "cool enough" to sit with her at the assembly. Did McKenzie bully Josie? Yes or No ――――――――――――――― *BULLYING BEHAVIOR TIC-TAC-TOE CARDS* © 2006 MAR*CO PRODUCTS, INC. 1-800-448-2197	Carmen invited the whole class to her end-of-the-school-year party. Did Carmen bully her classmates? Yes or No ――――――――――――――― *BULLYING BEHAVIOR TIC-TAC-TOE CARDS* © 2006 MAR*CO PRODUCTS, INC. 1-800-448-2197
Tenesha told Kasha to stop talking with Karli if she wants to still be Tenesha's friend. Did Tenesha bully Kasha? Yes or No ――――――――――――――― *BULLYING BEHAVIOR TIC-TAC-TOE CARDS* © 2006 MAR*CO PRODUCTS, INC. 1-800-448-2197	Tom told Kevin he could join the ballgame. Did Tom bully Kevin? Yes or No ――――――――――――――― *BULLYING BEHAVIOR TIC-TAC-TOE CARDS* © 2006 MAR*CO PRODUCTS, INC. 1-800-448-2197

I DIDN'T KNOW I WAS A BULLY © 2006 MAR*CO PRODUCTS, INC. 1-800-448-2197

Tori threatened to tell the teacher that Kailey cheated if Kailey didn't show her the answers on the math test. Did Tori bully Kailey? Yes or No ___ **BULLYING BEHAVIOR TIC-TAC-TOE CARDS** © 2006 MAR∗CO PRODUCTS, INC. 1-800-448-2197	Melanie passed a "popularity notebook" around for the "cool people" to sign. Did Melanie bully her classmates? Yes or No ___ **BULLYING BEHAVIOR TIC-TAC-TOE CARDS** © 2006 MAR∗CO PRODUCTS, INC. 1-800-448-2197
Kate three-way called Mary and Jen, but didn't tell Mary that Jen was on the line. Kate asked Mary if she liked Jen. Did Kate bully Mary? Yes or No ___ **BULLYING BEHAVIOR TIC-TAC-TOE CARDS** © 2006 MAR∗CO PRODUCTS, INC. 1-800-448-2197	Kevin told Martin he had to give him a dollar the next day or Kevin would beat him up. Did Kevin bully Martin? Yes or No ___ **BULLYING BEHAVIOR TIC-TAC-TOE CARDS** © 2006 MAR∗CO PRODUCTS, INC. 1-800-448-2197
Sam told Jarod he had to let him copy his homework or Sam would embarrass him in front of the whole class. Did Sam bully Jarod? Yes or No ___ **BULLYING BEHAVIOR TIC-TAC-TOE CARDS** © 2006 MAR∗CO PRODUCTS, INC. 1-800-448-2197	Jarod asked Tony if he needed help studying for a test. Did Jarod bully Tony? Yes or No ___ **BULLYING BEHAVIOR TIC-TAC-TOE CARDS** © 2006 MAR∗CO PRODUCTS, INC. 1-800-448-2197
Corey called Eric "four-eyes." Did Corey bully Eric? Yes or No ___ **BULLYING BEHAVIOR TIC-TAC-TOE CARDS** © 2006 MAR∗CO PRODUCTS, INC. 1-800-448-2197	Natasha's best friend Renee told Natasha she had to play what Renee wanted her to play at recess. Was Renee a bully to Natasha? Yes or No ___ **BULLYING BEHAVIOR TIC-TAC-TOE CARDS** © 2006 MAR∗CO PRODUCTS, INC. 1-800-448-2197
Tom tore Aaron's glider apart on purpose. Did Tom bully? Yes or No ___ **BULLYING BEHAVIOR TIC-TAC-TOE CARDS** © 2006 MAR∗CO PRODUCTS, INC. 1-800-448-2197	Karli wrote mean words about Melissa on her desk. Did Karli bully Melissa? Yes or No ___ **BULLYING BEHAVIOR TIC-TAC-TOE CARDS** © 2006 MAR∗CO PRODUCTS, INC. 1-800-448-2197

Lance laughed when Jeff put Doug down. Did Lance support Jeff in bullying? Yes or No ─────────────── *BULLYING BEHAVIOR TIC-TAC-TOE CARDS* © 2006 MAR∗CO PRODUCTS, INC. 1-800-448-2197	Karen asked Beth to join her and Amanda at the skating rink. Did Karen bully Beth? Yes or No ─────────────── *BULLYING BEHAVIOR TIC-TAC-TOE CARDS* © 2006 MAR∗CO PRODUCTS, INC. 1-800-448-2197
Carmen called Fred "stupid" because Fred didn't know the answer to the teacher's question. Did Carmen bully Fred? Yes or No ─────────────── *BULLYING BEHAVIOR TIC-TAC-TOE CARDS* © 2006 MAR∗CO PRODUCTS, INC. 1-800-448-2197	Justin punched Samuel in the stomach and called him names. Did Justin bully Samuel? Yes or No ─────────────── *BULLYING BEHAVIOR TIC-TAC-TOE CARDS* © 2006 MAR∗CO PRODUCTS, INC. 1-800-448-2197
Gabrielle asked Tawny not to talk about her friend Kim. Did Gabrielle bully Tawny? Yes or No ─────────────── *BULLYING BEHAVIOR TIC-TAC-TOE CARDS* © 2006 MAR∗CO PRODUCTS, INC. 1-800-448-2197	─────────────── *BULLYING BEHAVIOR TIC-TAC-TOE CARDS* © 2006 MAR∗CO PRODUCTS, INC. 1-800-448-2197
─────────────── *BULLYING BEHAVIOR TIC-TAC-TOE CARDS* © 2006 MAR∗CO PRODUCTS, INC. 1-800-448-2197	─────────────── *BULLYING BEHAVIOR TIC-TAC-TOE CARDS* © 2006 MAR∗CO PRODUCTS, INC. 1-800-448-2197
─────────────── *BULLYING BEHAVIOR TIC-TAC-TOE CARDS* © 2006 MAR∗CO PRODUCTS, INC. 1-800-448-2197	─────────────── *BULLYING BEHAVIOR TIC-TAC-TOE CARDS* © 2006 MAR∗CO PRODUCTS, INC. 1-800-448-2197

USE THE BLANK CARDS TO WRITE ADDITIONAL SITUATIONS RELEVANT TO YOUR GROUP/CLASS.

BULLYING WORD SEARCH CENTER INSTRUCTIONS

You will find copies of the *Bullying Word Search* and pencils at your center.

Here's what you are to do:

1. Each partner should take a copy of the *Bullying Word Search* and a pencil.

2. Complete the word search by finding the words at the top of the page. Look for answers vertically, horizontally, and diagonally. When you find a word, circle it and cross that word off your list.

3. Do not work with your partner. But if you get stumped, your partner might help you if you ask in a friendly way!

4. When you and your partner have completed the word search, compare your answers and put your activity sheets into your folders.

BULLYING WORD SEARCH KEY

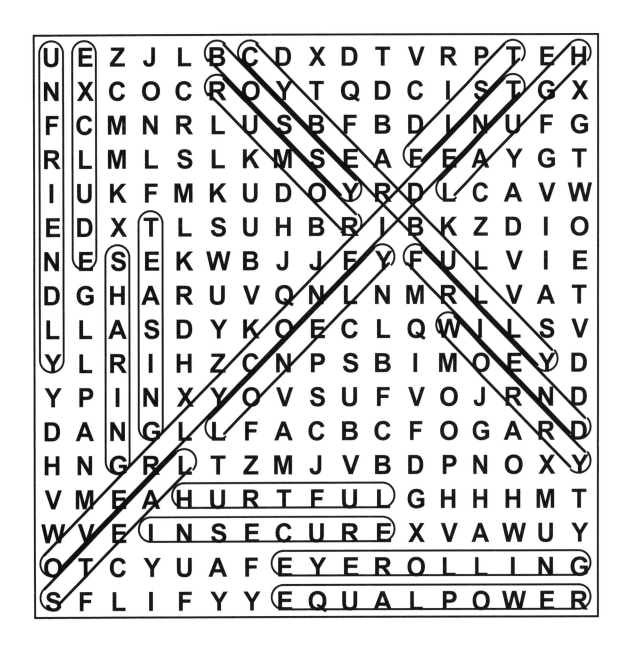

BULLYING WORD SEARCH

BOSSY
EXCLUDE
FRIEND
LAUGH
RUMOR
TEASING

CYBERBULLY
EYEROLLING
HURTFUL
LONELY
SHARING
UNFRIENDLY

EQUAL POWER
FIST
INSECURE
OVERLY CONFIDENT
STEAL
WORRY

```
U E Z J L B C D X D T V R P T E H
N X O C R O Y T Q D C I S T G X
F C M N R L U S B F B D I N U F G
R L M L S L K M S E A F E A Y G T
I U K F M K U D O Y R D L C A V W
E D X T L S U H B R I B K Z D I O
N E S E K W B J J F Y F U L V I E
D G H A R U V Q N L N M R L V A T
L L A S D Y K O E C L Q W I L S V
Y L R I H Z C N P S B I M O E Y D
Y P I N X Y O V S U F V O J R N D
D A N G L L F A C B C F O G A R D
H N G R L T Z M J V B D P N O X Y
V M E A H U R T F U L G H H H M T
W V E I N S E C U R E X V A W U Y
O T C Y U A F E Y E R O L L I N G
S F L I F Y Y E Q U A L P O W E R
```

BULLYING CROSSWORD PUZZLE CENTER INSTRUCTIONS

You will find copies of the *Bullying Crossword Puzzle* and pencils at your center.

Here's what you are to do:

1. Each partner should take a copy of the *Bullying Crossword Puzzle* and a pencil.

2. You may complete the puzzle by yourself or work with your partner. Sometimes two heads are better than one!

3. When you have completed the puzzle, compare your answers with your partner's and put your activity sheets into your folders.

BULLYING CROSSWORD PUZZLE KEY

BULLYING CROSSWORD PUZZLE

Across
1. A bully might tell you what to do or _____ you around.
4. A bully might send you a negative message on this.
7. A bully who does this might scare you.
9. A bully might make you do this instead of doing your work.
10. A bully might do this to you to make others laugh.
12. A bully might not do this with his/her friends.
14. A bully might not let you sit with him/her at this time.
15. A bully isn't a good one.

Down
2. A bully might make you feel this way when he/she threatens you.
3. A bully might be this person.
5. A bully might spread these about you.
6. A bully might do this to your lunch money.
8. A bully might roll these at you.
11. A bully might leave you out or do this to you.
13. A bully might make you let him/her copy this.
14. A bully might do this when you make a mistake.
15. A bully might shove this in your face.

BULLYING FILMSTRIP CENTER INSTRUCTIONS

You will find copies of the blank *Filmstrip* page, crayons, markers, and pencils at your center.

Here's what you are to do:

1. Each partner should choose a filmstrip theme and create a filmstrip about some kind of bullying. Possible themes are:

    A student being excluded from an activity
    A student being teased
    A student being cyberbullied
    A friend bullying another friend
    A bully threatening a student
    A student being bullied by rumors

2. Before beginning to draw, decide what will happen in your film and what picture you want in each box. You may ask your partner for ideas. Brainstorming with your partner may turn your filmstrip into a masterpiece!

3. Tell your story picture by picture. Remember to use color. Title your filmstrip at the top of the page and write your name to show that you are the originator of the film.

4. When you have completed your filmstrip, show it to your partner and put your activity sheet into your folder.

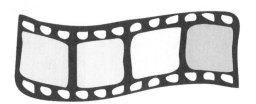

A FILMSTRIP BY _____

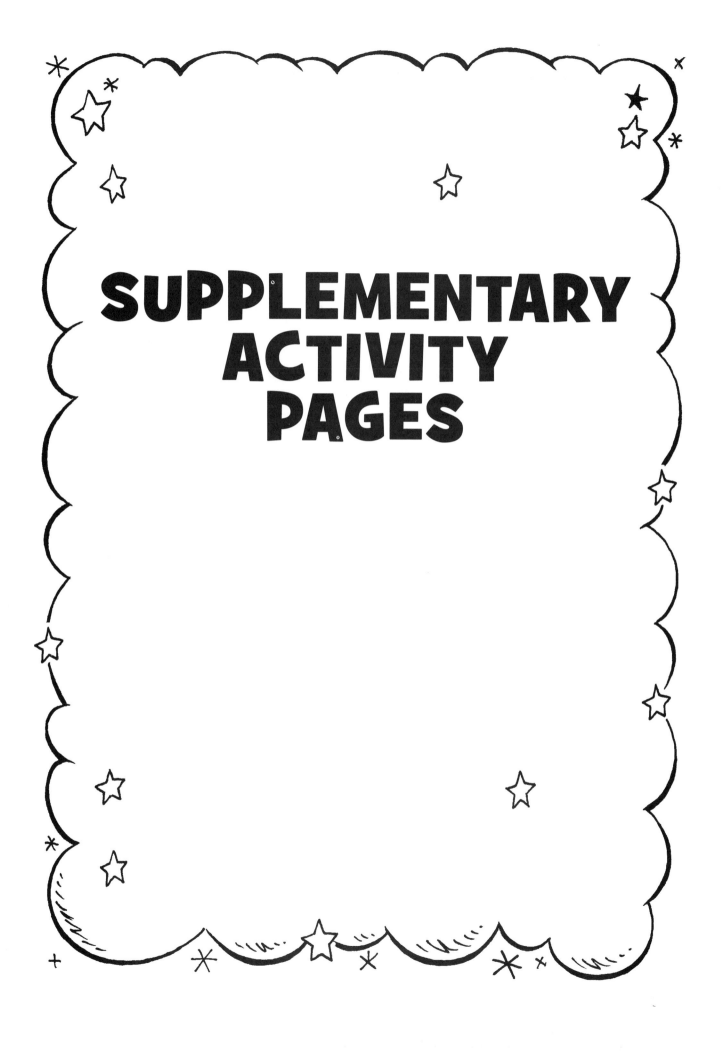

SUPPLEMENTARY PAGE INSTRUCTIONS/SUGGESTIONS

Lesson 1:

Behavior Survey (page 110). Make a copy for each student. Have the students complete the survey. Discuss the surveys or use it as a baseline indication of behavior. You may have the students complete the survey again at a later date to monitor their progress.

Teasing/Laughing (page 104). Make a copy for each student to color in order to reinforce the lesson about bullying behaviors.

I Don't Want To Be A Bully Rap (page 98). Make a copy for each student to recite with the group or students may volunteer to perform for the class.

Bullies, Bullies, Everywhere (page 99). Make a copy for each student to sing with the group or students may volunteer to perform for the class.

Lesson 2:

Excluding (page 105). Make a copy for each student to color in order to reinforce the lesson about bullying behaviors.

Bullying Behavior Grid (pages 100-101). Prepare the envelopes. Make a copy of the grid for each student. Have one student choose four letters and four place cards. Draw a sample grid on the board and write the selected letters and places on the grid. Have the students choose bullying situations, statements, behaviors, etc. that correspond to the letters and places chosen. Be prepared to help, if needed. This activity helps students understand where bullying occurs and what kind of bullying behaviors are exhibited at school. An added bonus is that this activity may point out bully situations you didn't know were present in your school.

Lesson 3:

Friendship Bullying (page 106). Make a copy for each student to color in order to reinforce the lesson about bullying behaviors.

Hidden Bullying Message (page 102). Make a copy for each student. Have the students complete the math problems to find the sum. Then have them use the sum to find the corresponding letter. The letter should be placed in the square under the problem. When the activity sheet is completed, the letters will reveal the hidden message on bullying.

Answer: I didn't know I was a bully!

Lesson 4:

Cyberbullying (page 107). Make a copy for each student to color in order to reinforce the lesson about bullying behaviors.

Bullying Skit Prompts (page 103). Divide the class into small groups and assign each group a skit prompt. Ask the students to design a skit that shows effective and ineffective ways to deal with a bully. Allow the students to present their skits to the class. Skits may also be used to help students in other classes learn about bullying.

Lesson 5:

Behavior-Change Plan (page 108). Make a copy for each student. Use this activity to help students target and change behaviors. Students may share their plans with the class or with a partner. Students' progress should be checked at a future date.

Behavior-Change Log (page 109). Make a copy for each student. This activity is used to track behavior changes and progress.

Lesson 6:

This lesson includes several games and activities which can be used at learning centers. The directions for each of these games and activities can be found following Lesson 6.

BULLYING BEHAVIOR GRID

Reproduce the *Place Cards.* Cut the cards apart and put them into an envelope. Reproduce and cut apart the *Letter Cards*. Put them into a second envelope. Have a student draw four cards from each envelope. Distribute a *Bullying Behavior Grid* activity sheet to each student. Draw a sample on the board. Write the chosen letters and places on the sample and instruct students to copy your sample onto their grids. The objective is to think of bullying behaviors beginning with the chosen letters that occur at the chosen places. Once students have completed the grid, have them share their answers with the class. Then discuss how to stop each of the bullying behaviors. (Examples: name-calling on the bus, hitting in the bathroom, laughing at someone in class, rolling your eyes at someone in the lunchroom)

S	C	R
N	T	P
H	L	J
M	F	S

- Lunchroom
- Bus
- Bathroom
- Recess
- Home
- Classroom
- Computer

BULLYING BEHAVIOR GRID

	LETTER:	LETTER:	LETTER:	LETTER:
PLACE:				
PLACE:				
PLACE:				
PLACE:				

HIDDEN BULLYING MESSAGE

Directions: Solve the following math problems. Use the answers to decode the hidden bullying message.

A	B	C	D	E	F	G	H	I	J	K	L	M	N	O	P	Q	R	S	T	U	V	W	X	Y	Z
1	2	3	4	5	6	7	8	9	10	11	12	13	14	15	16	17	18	19	20	21	22	23	24	25	26

11-2=___

7-3=___   6+3=___   10-6=___   6+8=___ ,   14+6=___

6+5=___   18-4=___   10+5=___   30-7=___   18-9=___

18+5=___   7-6=___   12+7=___   25-24=___

8-6=___   10+11=___   7+5=___   17-5=___   19+6=___ !

102 I DIDN'T KNOW I WAS A BULLY © 2006 MAR*CO PRODUCTS, INC. 1-800-448-2197

BULLYING SKIT PROMPTS

Divide the class into small groups. Give each group a skit prompt and ask the students to write a skit and be prepared to perform it. Ask the students to show ineffective and effective ways to deal with a bully. Allow time in class for writing and preparation. Emphasize that each member of the group should have *equal* participation in the project.

Skit prompts:

A student is excluded from an activity.

A student is teased.

A student is cyberbullied.

A friend is bullying another friend.

A bully threatens a student.

A student is bullied by rumors.

TEASING/LAUGHING

No one enjoys being laughed at or teased. Don't make jokes about others or laugh when others tease. Be considerate and don't join in any teasing. Be a good role model and show friends how **NOT** to be a bully.

EXCLUDING

Excluding others (leaving them out on purpose) is *bullying*. No one likes to feel unwanted. Always try to include others to help them feel accepted and important. You never know, you might be in their shoes one day!

FRIENDSHIP BULLYING

Keep "friendship power" equal. Do not try to order your friends around or boss them. Do not tell your friends whom they can sit beside, play with, or have as friends. Do not call friends names or make fun of them. Treat your friends like you want to be treated, as EQUALS.

CYBERBULLYING

Don't write unkind things about others on the computer or in notes. Spreading rumors or lies is *bullying*. Before you say or write anything about anyone, ask yourself, "Would I want this said or written about me?"

BEHAVIOR-CHANGE PLAN

NAME: _____ DATE: _____

The behavior I want to change is_____

_____ .

I feel _____ about this behavior, and I want to change it

because _____

_____ .

I have a plan to change this behavior.

I will _____

_____

_____

_____

_____ .

I will keep track of my behavior by _____

_____ .

BEHAVIOR-CHANGE LOG

Name: _____

Behavior to change: _____

Date: [_____]

My behavior ☐ improved ☐ stayed the same ☐ worsened

I feel _____ about my behavior.

I will _____ to improve my behavior.

Others will see me _____.

I will feel _____. **I can do it!**

Date: [_____]

My behavior ☐ improved ☐ stayed the same ☐ worsened

I feel _____ about my behavior.

I will _____ to improve my behavior.

Others will see me _____.

I will feel _____. **I can do it!**

Date: [_____]

My behavior ☐ improved ☐ stayed the same ☐ worsened

I feel _____ about my behavior.

I will _____ to improve my behavior.

Others will see me _____.

I will feel _____. **I can do it!**

I DIDN'T KNOW I WAS A BULLY © 2006 MAR★CO PRODUCTS, INC. 1-800-448-2197

BEHAVIOR SURVEY

Name: _____

Read each statement and mark your response in the square. Be honest with your answers. You will not be required to share your answers with your classmates.

	NEVER	SOMETIMES	OFTEN
1. I make physical threats to others.	☐	☐	☐
2. I tell others they cannot sit by me.	☐	☐	☐
3. I take things from other people.	☐	☐	☐
4. I talk to my friends in a bossy way.	☐	☐	☐
5. I roll my eyes at others.	☐	☐	☐
6. I tell some people we cannot be friends.	☐	☐	☐
7. I leave others out of games and activities.	☐	☐	☐
8. I write notes about other people.	☐	☐	☐
9. I spread rumors about others.	☐	☐	☐
10. I write about others on the Internet.	☐	☐	☐
11. I make fun of others.	☐	☐	☐
12. I laugh when someone is teased.	☐	☐	☐

MELISSA CRAWFORD RICHARDS

Melissa has a bachelor's degree in psychology and a master's degree in school counseling. She has been an elementary school counselor for 12 years with the New Albany-Floyd County School Corporation in southern Indiana. She has taught as an adjunct professor in the counseling department at Indiana University Southeast and has served as a mentor for many practicum and internship students. She believes that being a school counselor is the most rewarding occupation possible. Problem solving, teaching, comforting, supporting, assisting, caring, sharing, and mentoring make her school days feel short, but quite worthwhile.